Mahatma Gandhi

The Power of Peace

By Alan Trussell-Cullen

HAMERAY
PUBLISHING GROUP

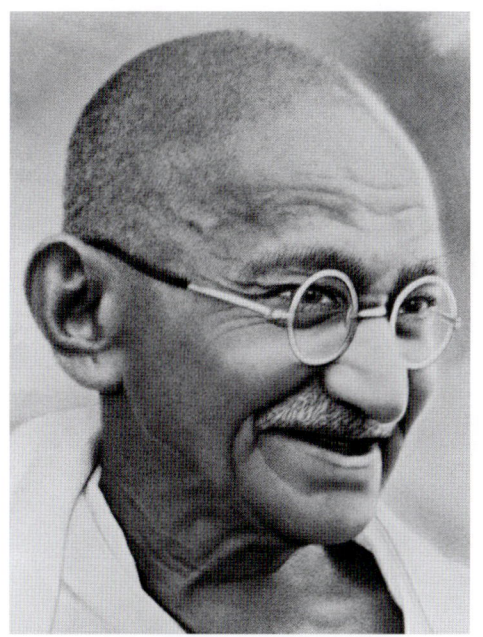

Published in the United States of America
by the Hameray Publishing Group, Inc.

Text © 2009, 2013 Alan Trussell-Cullen
Maps © 2009 Hameray Publishing Group, Inc.
First Published 2009
Revised Edition 2013

Publisher: Raymond Yuen
Series Editors: Adria F. Klein and Alan Trussell-Cullen
Project Editor: Kaitlyn Nichols
Designers: Lois Stanfield and Linda Lockowitz
Map Designer: Barry Age

Photo Credits: AP: pages 8, 13
Corbis: front cover and pages 1, 17, 18, 25, 32
Getty: back cover and pages 4, 10, 21, 22, 23, 29, 31

All rights reserved. No part of this publication may be reproduced or transmitted in any form or by any means without permission in writing from the publisher. Reproduction of any part of this book, through photocopy, recording, or any electronic or mechanical retrieval system without the written permission of the publisher, is an infringement of the copyright law.

ISBN 978-1-60559-064-6

Printed in Singapore

2 3 4 5 6 CP 17 16 15 14 13

Contents

Chapter 1	**Changing the Course of History**	5
Chapter 2	**Gandhi's Early Life**	7
Chapter 3	**Fighting for Indian Civil Rights in Southern Africa**	12
Chapter 4	**The Struggle for a Free India**	16
Chapter 5	**Spinning to Help People Help Themselves**	20
Chapter 6	**The Great Salt March**	24
Chapter 7	**One Country or Two?**	27
Chapter 8	**Gandhi's Legacy**	32
Timeline		34
Glossary		36
Learn More		38
Index		39

Chapter 1

Changing the Course of History

Mahatma Gandhi was born in India in 1869. At the time nearly a fifth of the world's population lived in India. But the Indian people did not rule their country. For three hundred years, the British had ruled India and much of the country's wealth ended up in the hands of the British. The Indian people struggled to be free, but the British had a powerful army and controlled India with many unfair laws.

◀ **Mahatma Gandhi dressed in traditional Indian cotton clothes.**

But one man found a weapon that could defeat even the strongest army and the toughest laws. That weapon was the power of peaceful protest. The man who taught his people how to use this power was Mahatma Gandhi. And he changed the course of history.

> *"When I despair, I remember that all through history the ways of truth and love have always won. There have been tyrants and murderers, and for a time they can seem invincible, but in the end they always fall."*
> —Mahatma Gandhi

Chapter 2

Gandhi's Early Life

Mohandas Gandhi was born in Porbandar (*pawr-buhn-der*) in western India on October 2, 1869. He was given the name "Mahatma" much later in his life in recognition of his work.

At first, Gandhi struggled with his school work. But he worked hard and became a very good student. Many of his important ideas came from reading.

> *"Live as if you were to die tomorrow. Learn as if you were to live forever."* —Mahatma Gandhi

▲ Mahatma Gandhi and his wife, Kasturba, in 1915.

In India it was the **custom** for parents to arrange marriages for their children. Gandhi's parents arranged for him to marry Kasturba (*kus-TOOR-ba*) when they were both thirteen. Marrying very young was part of the custom, too. Although they were only teenagers, they grew to love and respect each other and were married for sixty-two years.

> *Mahatma Gandhi and his wife Kasturba had four sons. Harilal was born in 1888, Manilal was born in 1892, Ramdas was born in 1898, and Gandhi himself helped deliver his youngest son, Devadas, in 1900.*

At the age of nineteen, Gandhi sailed to England to study to become a lawyer. His first son had just been born. His wife and son stayed behind in India. Gandhi's mother worried about how Gandhi, a Hindu, would

▲ Gandhi at age nineteen.

cope with the stress of living so far away from home. Gandhi told her not to worry.
He promised her he would stay true to his Hindu faith. This meant he did not eat meat or drink alcohol.

Hinduism

Hinduism is one of the world's oldest religions. Today there are over 900 million people throughout the world who follow Hinduism. Hindus do not eat meat because they believe that all living things, including animals, are sacred. They also do not drink alcohol.

Gandhi passed his final law exams in July 1891. It was time to return to India and to his wife and son.

Chapter 3

Fighting for Indian Civil Rights in Southern Africa

Back in India, Gandhi tried to work as a lawyer but at the start he wasn't very successful. In one of his first court cases he was so scared that he couldn't bring himself to speak. But Gandhi and his wife now had two sons to care for. So when a friend offered him a job as a lawyer in southern Africa for a year, Gandhi took it.

Southern Africa was a shock to Gandhi. In the 1890s white **settlers** were in charge. They treated the native Africans and the small numbers of the Indian population as **inferior** people. Treating people unfairly because of their race is called **racism**.

▲ Gandhi (center) in front of his law office in Johannesburg.

Gandhi had his first experience with racism the day he arrived. He had bought a first class ticket on a train, but when a white person got on board, Gandhi was forced to get off.

Gandhi thought the Indians in Africa should fight for their rights. He wrote letters to newspapers. When Indian workers were not treated fairly, he argued for them in court. In this way, he was able to use his skills as a lawyer and become more confident.

When Gandhi's job ended, he decided to stay in southern Africa, and his wife and family came to join him. In 1903 Gandhi started his own law office in Johannesburg. He defended many Indians against the government's racist laws. He was becoming a real leader. Gandhi hoped that life would get better for Indian people in Africa. But it didn't. The government passed a new law that said all Indians had to carry a **pass**, or special certificate, saying who they were at all times. If they didn't, they were put in prison or **deported**. Gandhi said the best way to fight unjust laws like this was to disobey them—but without using violence. Gandhi didn't believe in violence.

> *Gandhi made up a special word for disobeying the law in a peaceful way. He called it* satyagraha (sat-ya-gra-ha). *It means "the force of truth."*

Gandhi led the Indian people in a peaceful protest. They refused to carry their passes. Thousands of people, including Gandhi, were put in jail. But when news about the unrest began to spread around the world, the government was **embarrassed** and decided to change some of their unfair laws. It was the first victory for Gandhi's peaceful disobedience.

But Gandhi and his family had now been away from India for twenty-one years. They were homesick. In July 1914, they returned home.

Chapter 4

The Struggle for a Free India

When Gandhi arrived back in India he was already famous. People called him "Mahatma" which means "great soul." This name would be associated with him for the rest of his life and beyond.

The Indian people wanted him to lead them in their struggle against the British. Gandhi's peaceful disobedience, or *satyagraha*, had worked in Africa. They thought it would work in India, too.

Gandhi began by calling for a *hartal* (*hahr-TAHL*). This was a kind of general strike. Across India, people refused to work. Stores stayed closed. The country came to a standstill.

The British put people in prison for protesting but soon they didn't have enough prisons for all the people who were taking part in the protests.

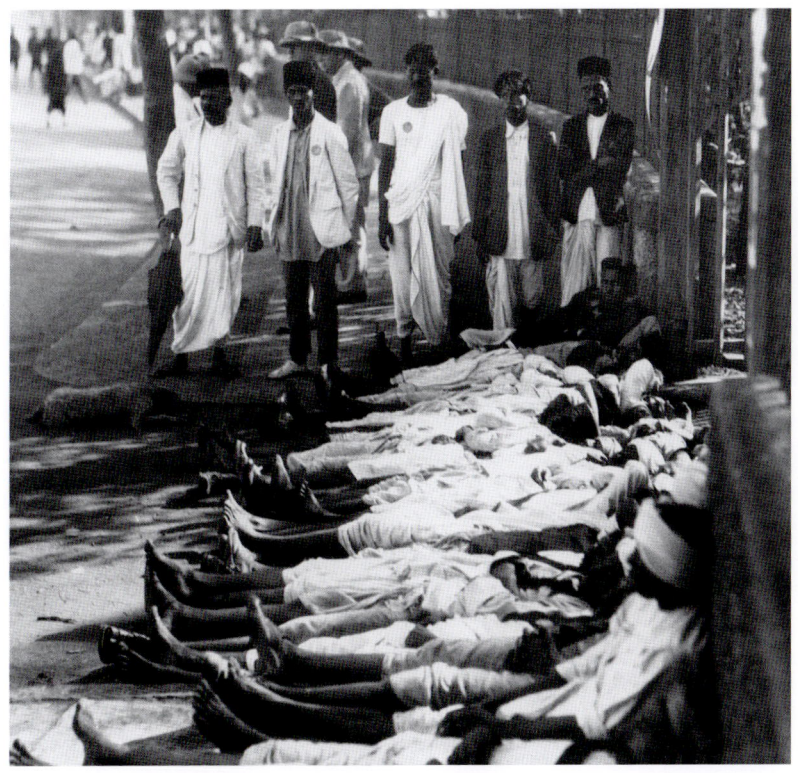

▲ Striking workers in India lay outside of their factory to protest against unfair British laws.

Most people protested peacefully. But in some cities, riots broke out. Gandhi was upset by this. He decided he would **fast**, or go without food, until people went back to protesting peacefully. Gandhi's fast worked. The people didn't want Gandhi to die, so the riots stopped and peace returned.

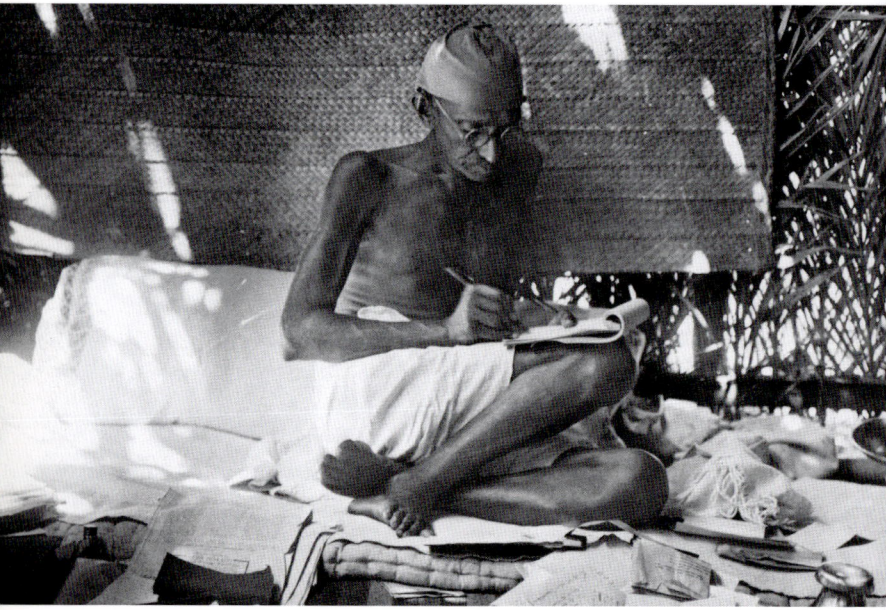

▲ Even when fasting, Gandhi continued to read, write, and study.

On April 13, 1919, a peaceful meeting was held in Amritsar (*uhm-RIT-ser*). It was a religious holiday and everyone was in a festive mood. But General Dyer, the local British commander, was furious about the meeting. Without warning, he ordered his soldiers to start shooting into the crowd. In ten minutes they had killed 379 people and wounded 7,200 more.

The Amritsar Massacre shocked the world. It made Gandhi all the more determined to fight against the British. He joined a political group called the Indian National Congress. In October 1921 the group called on all Indian government workers to strike. Again, Gandhi's protests brought the country to a standstill.

The British tried to fight this by putting people in prison. More than twenty thousand people including Gandhi were put in prison. Gandhi would remain in prison for six long years. But nothing the British did seemed to stop the growing **rebellion** in India.

Chapter 5

Spinning to Help People Help Themselves

For years the British had been buying cotton from Indian farmers for a very low price. They would ship it back to England where it was spun into cotton thread and made into cotton cloth. This was made into western-style clothes which the British then sold to people in India for a high price.

Gandhi saw how this was keeping his people poor. He told them to spin their own cotton and make their own traditional clothes. Gandhi set an example to people by doing this himself. Every day he sat at his spinning wheel to spin two hundred yards of cotton. Even in prison he continued to spin his own cotton.

People all over India began to spin their own cotton and make their own clothes.

▲ Gandhi working next to his spinning wheel.

▲ The spinning wheel appears on the country's flag as a symbol of the new India.

Gandhi also worked hard to help the poorest people in India. At that time they were called the "Untouchables." That was because for centuries India had a **caste system**. Everyone was born into a particular caste, or group. The caste of people determined how important they were. People born into the lowest caste were thought to be so low that others would not even touch them.

Gandhi wanted to help poor people called ▶ "untouchable" like this family living in Calcutta.

Throughout his life, Gandhi worked to help the Untouchables and to teach others to treat them with equality. He hated the name Untouchables, so he gave them a new name. He called them *Harijans* or "Children of God." If he came across people treating these people unfairly, Gandhi would go without food and fast until the people changed their ways. Years later, when India became independent, the constitution of the country would make it illegal to treat people as untouchable.

Chapter 6

The Great Salt March

One way to show the British that the Indian people wanted to rule themselves was to stop paying taxes to Britain. One of the most hated taxes in India was the British tax on salt. The British wouldn't let anyone in India make their own salt. Everyone needed salt, so everyone had to pay the salt tax.

In 1930, as a protest against the salt tax, Gandhi set out to walk two hundred miles to the ocean on his Great Salt March. Along the way he told people he was going to make his own salt and break the law. Thousands joined his march.

Gandhi on the Great Salt March. ▶

The British were puzzled. They didn't know how Gandhi was going to make salt. When Gandhi and his followers got to the ocean, he put his hands in the water and then held them up to the sun. The sun dried the saltwater, leaving some grains of salt on his hands. Gandhi's **symbolic action** had broken the law. He had made his own salt.

Throughout India, people began to make their own salt from the sea. Again, the British tried to stop them by putting them in prison. Soon there were over sixty thousand people in prison. Finally the British government had to give in and let the Indian people make their own salt.

> *"A small body of determined spirits fired by an unquenchable faith in their mission can alter the course of history."*
> —Mahatma Gandhi

Chapter 7

One Country or Two?

After the Second World War, the British government changed. The new British government was ready to let India rule itself. All the peaceful protests Gandhi had helped lead had worked. But there were still problems.

There were many religious groups in India but two of the main ones were Hindus and Muslims. Gandhi was a Hindu but he had great respect for Muslims. Gandhi had always wanted India to be one country. But after the war the Muslim leaders decided they wanted India to be divided into two separate countries. India would be mainly for Hindus. A new country called Pakistan would be mainly for Muslims. Gandhi didn't like this. He thought people should be able to live together peacefully, regardless of their religious beliefs.

On August 15, 1947, the people of the two new countries, India and Pakistan, finally gained their independence from Britain. One fifth of the world's population suddenly became independent. But Gandhi was afraid that dividing India into two countries would lead to conflict.

Gandhi was right. When the boundaries for the two countries were drawn, thousands of Hindus found that they now lived in Pakistan where most people were Muslims. Thousands of Muslims found themselves living in India where most people were Hindus. People began to flee from one country to the other. In the months that followed, twelve million people fled in opposite directions. Violence broke out in many places and thousands of people were killed.

Gandhi was heartbroken. But he continued to work for peace. As he had done so many times before in his peaceful protests against the British, he stopped eating and fasted until people stopped their fighting.

Gandhi was now seventy-seven and weak from fasting. He still got up at 3:00 a.m. to start his day's work. Every evening he went back to his house to share evening prayers in the garden with anyone who wanted to come.

◀
Gandhi shared prayers in his garden every evening.

On the evening of January 30, 1948, Gandhi came into his garden. A crowd of three hundred people had gathered there. Gandhi smiled and waved to the people. But one man was not there for prayers. As Gandhi began to speak he took out a gun and shot him dead. Gandhi had been **assassinated**.

The prime minister of the new India broadcast the news to the country. "The light has gone out in our lives and there is darkness everywhere. Our beloved leader . . . the father of our nation, is no more . . . "

The whole country stopped for his funeral. One and a half million people marched in his funeral procession. Another million stood on the side of the road.

The streets of India were full of people mourning the loss of Gandhi. ▶

Chapter 8

Gandhi's Legacy

Gandhi's legacy was one of peace. He showed that peaceful protests could bring about great changes.

He inspired other great leaders for change around the world including Martin Luther King Jr. and Nelson Mandela. His way of living his life continues to inspire people today. Gandhi won freedom for his people. But he also taught people to care for others and to look after the world we live in.

Timeline

1869   Mohandas Gandhi is born in Porbandar, India on October 2

1882   Marries Kasturba

1888   Sails to England to study law

1893   Starts a new life in southern Africa; experiences racism and vows to fight it

1903   Starts his law practice in Johannesburg

1906   Launches his *satyagraha*, or nonviolent campaign, against racist laws in southern Africa

1914   Succeeds in getting the government in southern Africa to change some laws against Indians; later returns to India

1919   Launches a peaceful *hartal*; Amritsar Massacre occurs on April 1

1922 Imprisoned for six years for telling people to rebel against British rule

1930 Starts the Great Salt March, April 6

1946 Opposes the dividing of India into two countries

1947 India celebrates independence, August 15

1948 Violence breaks out; Gandhi fasts to try to stop it

1948 Gandhi is assassinated, January 30

Glossary

assassinated — killed by someone; the word is usually used when a leader or someone important has been killed

caste system — a system of social classes based on wealth, occupation, or race

custom — a common practice or way of doing things

deported — sent out of the country

embarrassed — made to feel uncomfortable

fast — to go without food

independent — when people or countries are free to manage and control themselves

inferior — not as good or as important

legacy — what people leave or achieve after their death

pass — a kind of official certificate that says who you are

racism — prejudice or discrimination based on a person's race

rebellion — refusal to accept the authority or rules set by the people in charge

settlers — people who have recently moved into an area and built houses on the land there

symbolic action — an action that carries a special meaning or significance

Learn More

Books

Gandhi by Primo Levi (DK Children, 2006)
Gandhi: Young Nation Builder
  by Kathleen Kiudlinski (Aladdin, 2006)
The Words of Gandhi by Richard Attenborough
  (Topeka Bindary, 2001)
World Peacemakers: Mahatma Gandhi by
  by Michael Nicholson (Blackbirch Press, 2003)

Websites

www.mkgandhi.org
www.mkgandhi.org/students/story1.htm
http://www.sscnet.ucla.edu/southasia/History/
  Gandhi/gandhi.html
www.time.com/time/time100/leaders/profile/
  gandhi.html

Movies

Gandhi The Oscar winning-movie starring
  Ben Kingsley (Sony Pictures, 1982)

Index

Africa 12, 14, 16
Amritsar 19, 33
Amritsar Massacre 19, 33
army 5, 6
assassinated 30, 36

boundaries 28
Britain 24, 28
British 5, 16, 17, 19, 20, 24, 26, 27, 29

caste system 22, 36
cotton 20, 21
custom 9, 36

deported 15, 36
disobedience 15, 16
Dyer, General 19

embarrassed 15, 36
England 9, 20
equality 23

faith 11
fast 18, 23, 29, 36
funeral 30

Great Salt March 24

Harijans 23
hartal 16
Hindu 9, 11, 27, 28

independent 23, 28
India 5, 7, 9, 11, 12, 15, 16, 19, 20, 21, 22, 23, 24, 26, 27, 28, 30, 33
Indian National Congress 19
inferior 12, 37

Johannesburg 14

Kasturba 9
King Jr., Martin Luther 32

laws 5, 6, 14, 15
lawyer 9, 12, 14
legacy 32, 37

Mandela, Nelson 32
Muslims 27, 28

native 12

Pakistan 27, 28
pass 14, 37
Porbandar 7, 33
prayers 29, 30
prime minister 30
protest 6, 15, 17, 18, 19, 24, 27, 29, 32

racism 12, 14, 37
rebellion 19, 37
religious beliefs 28
riots 18

satyagraha 15, 16
Second World War 27
settlers 12, 37
spinning wheel 20
strike 16, 19
symbolic action 26, 37

taxes 24

unrest 15
Untouchables 22, 23

violence 15, 28